JURASSIC

RECORD BREAKERS

DARREN NAISH

CARLTON
KIDS

 ## ABOUT THE AUTHOR

Dr Darren Naish is a palaeontologist and science writer specializing in dinosaurs and prehistoric creatures. When he's not busy digging up dinosaurs and ancient reptiles, he's writing about them! Darren is an Honorary Research Associate at the University of Portsmouth, UK.

New dinosaur discoveries are being made all the time, but there are still many things that we don't know about dinosaurs. Sometimes we can only make educated guesses about them, often by comparing dinosaurs with modern animals. For example, nobody is certain exactly how fast most dinosaurs could move, but experts can estimate their speed, based on how fast modern animals can run.

Dinosaur experts like Dr Naish sometimes need to use special words to describe dinosaurs, but you'll find these words explained in the glossary on page 46.

 # CONTENTS

RECORD-BREAKING DINOSAURS

Between 230 and 65 million years ago (mya), some of the most amazing creatures ever to have lived ruled our planet. The most successful of these were a group of reptiles that lived on land - the dinosaurs!

Dinosaurs reached record-breaking sizes and many grew amazing body armour, horns, spikes and claws. In this book, we look at the Jurassic period - a time ruled by some of the most amazing dinosaurs ever.

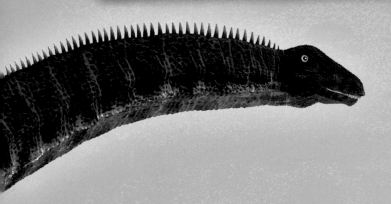

DINOSAURS RULE!

Dinosaurs were the most successful animals on land for about 165 million years. No other single group of animals has been so important for so long. By comparison, humans have been around for just a few million years.

WHERE ARE THEY NOW?

The reign of the dinosaurs did not last for ever. Sixty-five million years ago one of the biggest natural disasters of all time caused almost all of the dinosaurs to vanish. Dinosaurs didn't die out completely though: one group survived. We call them birds.

CHANGING PLANET

Dinosaurs appeared during the Triassic period about 230 mya, and they thrived and evolved during the following Jurassic and Cretaceous periods. Together, these three time periods are known as the Mesozoic Era (see below). The world underwent a huge number of changes during the Mesozoic Era and dinosaurs had to evolve to survive.

DINOSAUR TIMELINE

Dinosaurs and mammals evolve

Birds evolve

TRIASSIC PERIOD	JURASSIC PERIOD
250 mya	199 mya

145 mya

MESOZOIC ERA

🏆 DINOSAUR FAMILY TREE

One reason for the dinosaurs' record-breaking success was their ability to evolve (develop and change) very rapidly. Early in their history, dinosaurs split into two major groups: the beaked ornithischians ('or-nith-iss-key-ans') and the long-necked saurischians ('sore-iss-key-ans').

Both groups started out as small, two-legged animals with flexible necks, grabbing hands and slim legs. Over millions of years, dinosaurs became increasingly spectacular and record-breaking species evolved in both groups.

Ceratopsians   Pachycephalosaurs

Ornithopods

Stegosaurs   Ankylosaurs

Sauropods

Theropods

Herrerasaurids

Saurischians
Saurischians included the biggest dinosaurs of all (the long-necked sauropods) and the fearsome, meat-eating theropods.

Ornithischians
Ornithischians included record-breaking horned dinosaurs, spiky stegosaurs and the armour-plated ankylosaurs.

Dinosaurs

🏆 RIVAL REPTILES

Dinosaurs weren't the only prehistoric record breakers. Flying reptiles called pterosaurs and amazing marine reptiles shared the world with the dinosaurs and were also among the most amazing record breakers ever to evolve on Earth.

During the Triassic period the continents were united in a giant super-continent called Pangaea – the biggest landmass there has ever been. This allowed dinosaurs to spread far and wide across the planet.

TRIASSIC

Pangaea

During the Jurassic and Cretaceous periods Pangaea broke up into smaller continents with different climates and plants. In turn, groups of dinosaurs split up and evolved into new species to suit their new surroundings.

CRETACEOUS

North America   Asia

Africa

South America

Antarctica

Dinosaurs become extinct, but birds survive

Humans evolve

CRETACEOUS PERIOD

65 mya

Now

CENOZOIC ERA

SUPER HEAVYWEIGHT CHAMPION

AMPHICOELIAS

Plant-eating dinosaurs known as sauropods had extremely long tails and necks and were often enormous, but one giant called Amphicoelias (am-fee-see-lee-us) out-sized all the others.

Only two of this plant-eater's bones have been found so far, but scientists have used them to work out that it was the biggest land animal that ever lived.

Amphicoelias was so big that it would have had to feed on hundreds of kilograms of plant food every day. It must have lived in places where there were lots of shrubs and trees.

The sheer size of Amphicoelias would have protected it from most predators.

AMPHICOELIAS
(am-fee-see-lee-us)

WHEN	Jurassic 155-145 mya
WHERE	USA
SIZE	40-60m long
WEIGHT	About 70-100 tonnes
DIET	Herbivorous
SPEED	16km/h
DANGER	MEDIUM

BIGGER THAN A WHALE

Amphicoelias was longer than a blue whale, but not as heavy. With its long neck, this dinosaur was tall enough to reach the treetops to feed. Amphicoelias could even have stood on its hind legs to reach higher, using its tail as a prop. Then again, it was also strong enough to simply push the trees over. It would have certainly made the ground shake when it walked!

To get this big, Amphicoelias would have to spend a lot of its time eating, stripping the leaves off trees with its pencil-shaped teeth.

HOW HEAVY?

Awesome Amphicoelias weighed up to 100 tonnes - that's as much as 20 African elephants.

SUPERSIZE SAUROPOD

One of the Amphicoelias bones discovered is from the spine and is over 2 metres tall! Part of a thigh bone was also found. This piece of bone suggests that Amphicoelias had back legs that were up to 9 metres long - that's as tall as two giraffes.

10

5

0

metres

FIRST FOSSIL PREDATOR

MEGALOSAURUS

Megalosaurus (meg-al-oh-saw-rus) was the first ever dinosaur recognised by science. It was discovered in England over 300 years ago in the late 1700s.

Today we know that big predatory dinosaurs like Megalosaurus were two-legged animals with clawed, grabbing hands, but the scientists who first studied the bones were very puzzled by what they had found.

When Megalosaurus was first discovered, experts thought that its long, heavy tail dragged along the ground like that of a giant lizard. Later discoveries showed that the tails of just about all dinosaurs were actually held up in the air.

⬢ NUMBER ONE

A palaeontologist called William Buckland was the first person to study the remains of Megalosaurus and even gave the dinosaur its name. The remains were a mixture of bones belonging to several megalosaurs of different ages and sizes, including part of a lower jaw, with several of its curved, serrated teeth still in place. Buckland could see this new beast was a fierce predator, even if he didn't know exactly what it was.

⬢ THE FIRST DISCOVERIES

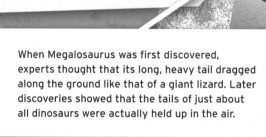

1824 ➡ MEGALOSAURUS
1825 ➡ IGUANODON
1833 ➡ HYLAEOSAURUS
1836 ➡ THECODONTOSAURUS
1837 ➡ PLATEOSAURUS

MEGALOSAURUS
(meg-al-oh-saw-rus)

WHEN	Jurassic 167-164 mya
WHERE	England
SIZE	6m long
WEIGHT	700kg
DIET	Carnivorous
SPEED	48km/h
DANGER	HIGH

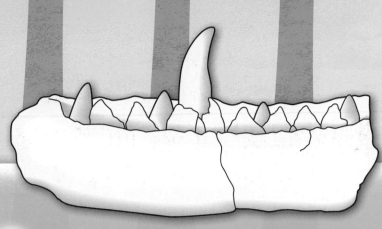

🦖 MEGA LIZARD

The lower jaw that was first found looked similar to the jaw bones of modern monitor lizards, so it was thought that Megalosaurus was shaped like a huge lizard walking on all fours. During the 1850s the 'giant lizard' idea gave way to the idea of a reptilian elephant, with four column-like legs and a short body and tail. Both were wrong.

Megalosaurus had powerful arms and may have used them to help keep prey animals still while it bit them.

🦖 BIG BITER

Fossils of other predatory dinosaurs, mostly from North America, eventually showed that Megalosaurus and its relatives were not lizard-shaped, nor did they walk on all fours. Instead they were two-legged predators with short arms and three large hand claws. They probably killed plant-eating dinosaurs by grabbing them with their clawed hands and taking slashing bites with their serrated teeth.

SMALLEST PREDATOR

ANCHIORNIS

At just 40 centimetres long, feathered Anchiornis (an-kee-orr-nis) from China holds the record for being the smallest known predatory dinosaur.

It would have weighed about 250 grams and was just over the size of a pigeon. A few other predatory dinosaurs – like Epidendrosaurus and Epidexipteryx – may have been smaller, but no fully grown adults have yet been found, so they can't qualify for the record.

MINI HUNTER

At first it was thought that Anchiornis was a type of ancient bird, but it's actually a bird-like dinosaur and a close relative of Troodon. Like most bird-like dinosaurs, it had long grasping hands and sharp, closely packed teeth. It was probably a speedy hunter of lizards and insects.

ANCHIORNIS
(an-kee-orr-nis)

WHEN	Jurassic 165-155 mya
WHERE	China
SIZE	40cm long
WEIGHT	250g
DIET	Carnivorous
SPEED	Up to 40km/h
DANGER	NONE

1 → ANCHIORNIS → ABOUT 40cm LONG
2 → PARVICURSOR → ABOUT 45cm LONG
3 → CAENAGNATHASIA → ABOUT 45cm LONG
4 → MEI LONG → ABOUT 45cm LONG
5 → MAHAKALA → ABOUT 50cm LONG

DINKY DRAGON

In recent years, scientists have found quite a few new tiny predators, mostly in China and Mongolia. One of these is named Mei long. It was only about 45 centimetres long and the only known specimen was preserved curled up, as if asleep. This explains its name - it means 'soundly sleeping dragon'.

Thanks to its small size and long feathers, Anchiornis could probably glide or flap its wings. It might have jumped around on tree branches.

Sharp teeth and a slender snout suggest that Anchiornis preyed on small lizards and large insects.

The three long, slender, clawed fingers were mostly hidden by long arm and hand feathers.

MOST FEARSOME SEA PREDATOR

LIOPLEURODON

Liopleurodon (lye-oh-pluur-oh-don) – a short-necked plesiosaur the size of a male sperm whale – wins the title of the ultimate ocean-going predator.

Bite marks preserved on fossil bones show that this sea monster attacked and ate other huge sea reptiles, sometimes biting them into pieces. Some experts calculate that its bite was perhaps ten times stronger than that of Tyrannosaurus rex!

The pointed, gently curved teeth were deep-rooted in the jaws. They were perfect for grabbing struggling prey and for cutting into flesh.

 **POWER BITE**

Liopleurodon probably took prey by surprise, rushing it at speed and attacking with an open mouth. It could have bitten off the paddles of other plesiosaurs, wrenching them clean off the body. Huge muscles at the back of its head powered its long, crocodile-like jaws. Its banana-shaped teeth were up to 30cm long.

GIANT KILLERS

Remains of Liopleurodon show that it definitely reached 6 metres in length, but small bits of fossilised bone from the lower jaw and back suggest that it could have been up to 15 metres long! By comparison, a modern-day killer whale is almost 10 metres long and the largest great white shark was 7 metres long.

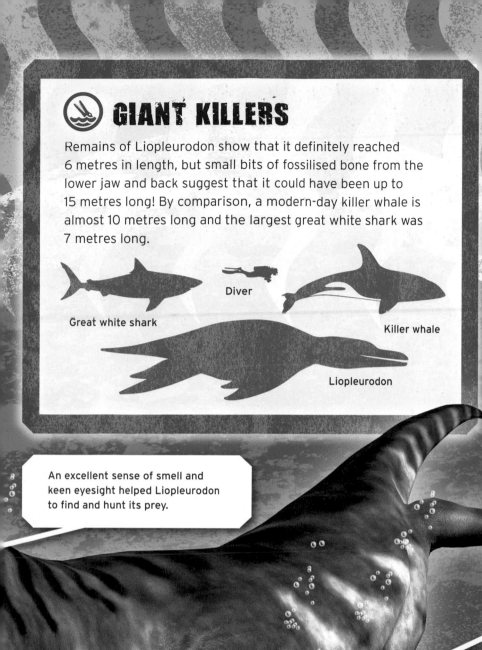

Great white shark

Diver

Killer whale

Liopleurodon

An excellent sense of smell and keen eyesight helped Liopleurodon to find and hunt its prey.

Fossilised stomach contents show that giant plesiosaurs such as Liopleurodon ate fish, swimming molluscs, other plesiosaurs, and the floating dead bodies of land animals like dinosaurs.

DEADLY AMBUSH

Because of its huge size, Liopleurodon would have taken care not to get stranded in shallow water. However, it may sometimes have taken a risk to catch prey. It is a very real possibility that it grabbed paddling dinosaurs and pulled them into deep water. Today, killer whales hunt in this way. They rush up beaches and snatch sea lion pups from the water's edge.

MOST VALUABLE

ARCHAEOPTERYX

The first bird ever found, Archaeopteryx (ar-kee-op-terr-ix), is one of the most valuable fossils of all time.

It is also one of the most important, since it was a crucial piece of evidence showing that birds evolved from small, predatory dinosaurs. Ten fossils have been found so far, and are regarded as the most valuable of all dinosaur finds. Specimens are worth around £10 million each.

 ## BEAUTIFULLY PRESERVED

Archaeopteryx lived near lagoons where the soft mud was perfect for preserving fossils. All of the Archaeopteryx specimens found so far were discovered in a layer of rock from one of these lagoons. This rock, called the Solnhofen limestone, is made up of tiny, smooth mud particles that once settled on the lagoon floor. The bodies of animals that fell in were beautifully preserved by the mud, revealing lots of fine detail, including feathers and teeth.

ARCHAEOPTERYX
(ar-kee-op-terr-ix)

WHEN	Jurassic 155-150 mya
WHERE	Germany
SIZE	50cm long
WEIGHT	500g
DIET	Carnivorous
SPEED	48km/h
DANGER	NONE

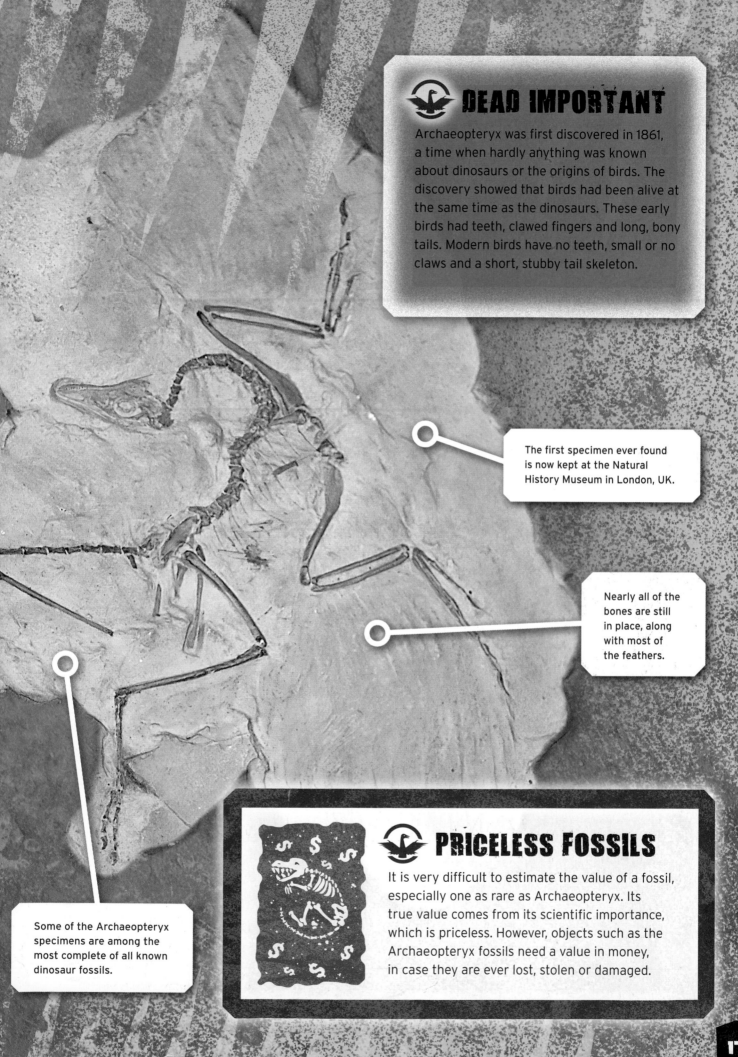

Archaeopteryx was first discovered in 1861, a time when hardly anything was known about dinosaurs or the origins of birds. The discovery showed that birds had been alive at the same time as the dinosaurs. These early birds had teeth, clawed fingers and long, bony tails. Modern birds have no teeth, small or no claws and a short, stubby tail skeleton.

The first specimen ever found is now kept at the Natural History Museum in London, UK.

Nearly all of the bones are still in place, along with most of the feathers.

Some of the Archaeopteryx specimens are among the most complete of all known dinosaur fossils.

PRICELESS FOSSILS

It is very difficult to estimate the value of a fossil, especially one as rare as Archaeopteryx. Its true value comes from its scientific importance, which is priceless. However, objects such as the Archaeopteryx fossils need a value in money, in case they are ever lost, stolen or damaged.

FASTEST TAIL

DIPLODOCUS

Giant sauropods like Diplodocus (dip-lo-doe-cus) had amazing tails. The end was highly flexible, skinny, and shaped like a bullwhip.

Some scientists believe its tail was actually used like a whip and that the tip could be swished at supersonic speeds. If true, dinosaurs were the first living things in history to break through the sound barrier!

A few fossilised patches of skin show that sauropods were covered in small, rounded scales, though some kinds had armour plates and short bony lumps as well.

TOP TO TAIL

We now know that Diplodocus and its relatives had a row of tall, triangular spines running along the top of the neck, back and tail. This spiky fringe - similar to that of modern iguanas - would have given these dinosaurs a more showy appearance than previously imagined.

DIPLODOCUS

(dip-lo-doe-cus)

WHEN	Jurassic 150-147 mya
WHERE	USA
SIZE	32m long
WEIGHT	30 tonnes
DIET	Herbivorous
SPEED	Up to 16km/h
DANGER	HIGH

FASTER THAN SOUND?

Some experts think that the tail-tip of Diplodocus could have been used to make a loud 'crack' to scare other dinosaurs or to attract a mate. A whip makes this noise when its tip travels at more than 1,206 kilometres per hour. The whip's tip breaks through the sound barrier and makes a small sonic boom, just as an aircraft does when it reaches similar speeds.

Many dinosaurs had powerful tails, but Diplodocus was exceptional. Enormous bony 'wings' sticking out from the sides of the tail bones anchored massive muscles. These allowed the tail to be thrashed from side to side.

LIVING WHIP

If Diplodocus did use its tail tip as a whip to lash out at an attacker, it would have had to be careful. Such heavy use could have snapped Diplodocus's tail or shredded it of its skin.

Sauropods like Diplodocus are usually imagined as 'gentle giants', but big modern plant-eaters such as rhinoceroses are often dangerous and aggressive. Diplodocus's giant size, powerful kick and enormous whiplash tail would have made it one of the most formidable creatures of the Jurassic period.

BIGGEST SHOW-OFF

STEGOSAURUS

Stegosaurus (steg-oh-saw-rus) had some of the most impressive structures ever found on an animal's body. These were probably used for 'showing off'.

Enormous diamond-shaped plates more than 70 centimetres tall and 80 centimetres wide grew from its neck, back and tail. It's even possible that they were brightly coloured.

 ### PUZZLING PLATES

Stegosaurus's plates weren't just made of bone. They also had a horny covering on top, but this has not survived in fossils. We know that this covering was living, growing material, but we don't know how big or what shape it was. These plates could have been even bigger than we imagine!

The plates stuck upwards and slightly outwards, so they would have been useless as body armour. Stegosaurus was about the size of a bus, so it probably relied on its size to defend itself.

PLAYING IT COOL?

Stegosaurus might have used its plates to control its body temperature. They could have absorbed the sun's heat to keep the dinosaur warm, or given off heat like a radiator, helping it to cool down when it was hot.

Most similar dinosaurs had pairs of plates in a row, but Stegosaurus plates were arranged in an alternating pattern.

The plates on the neck were small. The biggest plates were over the hips and base of the tail.

FASHION STATEMENT

There were several species of dinosaurs similar to Stegosaurus, such as Loricatosaurus (below), but they had smaller plates in different shapes. Perhaps different types of stegosaur had different-shaped plates. This might have helped them to tell each other apart, so they could show off to their own kind.

SMALLEST PLANT-EATER

FRUITADENS

The smallest plant-eater yet discovered is little Fruitadens (froot-ah-dens). A fully-grown adult was only about the size of a cat.

It ran on its back legs and used its teeth to mash up leaves and fruit. It might have used its claws to grab fruit and small lizards.

Small dinosaurs like Fruitadens had many predators. Its very long, flexible tail may have helped it to balance when running on its back legs, increasing the speed of its get-away.

 SMALL IS SMART?

DISADVANTAGES OF BEING SMALL

★ BIG ANIMALS OR BAD WEATHER CAN EASILY DESTROY A SMALL DINOSAUR'S HOME

★ IT TAKES A LOT OF EFFORT TO MOVE LONG DISTANCES

★ SMALL DINOSAURS OFTEN HAVE TO EAT A LOT FOR THEIR SIZE

★ EVEN SMALL ANIMALS LIKE LIZARDS AND BIG SPIDERS MIGHT BE A THREAT

ADVANTAGES OF BEING SMALL

★ SMALL DINOSAURS CAN EASILY HIDE FROM PREDATORS AND BAD WEATHER

★ SMALL DINOSAURS ONLY NEED A SMALL LIVING SPACE TO SLEEP IN

★ SMALL DINOSAURS CAN GET ALL THE FOOD THEY NEED FROM JUST TWO OR THREE TREES

★ SMALL DINOSAURS CAN FEED ON EASY-TO-FIND FOODS LIKE SMALL BUGS AND SEEDS

FRUITADENS
(froot-ah-dens)

WHEN	Jurassic 150 mya
WHERE	USA
SIZE	70cm long
WEIGHT	About 800g
DIET	Herbivorous or omnivorous
SPEED	Up to 40km/h
DANGER	LOW

 # MODERN-DAY MINI DINOS

Birds evolved in the Jurassic period from small predatory dinosaurs, so it could be said that really small dinosaurs are still alive today! Perhaps we should keep them in mind when talking about the record for the smallest dinosaur! This tiny Cuban bee hummingbird, for example, is just 5 centimetres long.

Tiny dinosaurs like Fruitadens would need to hide from big predators. They might have slept in burrows.

Fruitadens's body and tail may have been covered in long, hair-like fibres.

 ## FUNNY FANGS

Fruitadens belongs to a group of dinosaurs called the heterodontosaurs, which means 'different-toothed dinosaurs'. Their jaws had beaked tips, with teeth for chewing at the back. What makes them unusual is that they had fangs at the front, probably used for biting, fighting and showing off.

GIANT-EYED SEA REPTILE

OPHTHALMOSAURUS

Ichthyosaurs were dolphin-shaped marine reptiles that roamed the prehistoric seas. One ichthyosaur called Ophthalmosaurus (off-thal-moe-saw-rus) had huge eyes compared to the size of its body.

Though this creature was only 4 metres long, its eyeballs were an incredible 23 centimetres in width - that's about the size of a melon. Huge eyes like this probably evolved so that Ophthalmosaurus could see and hunt prey in deep water.

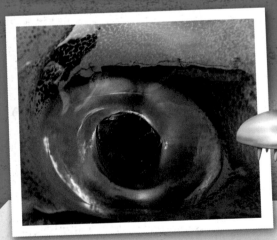

 NIGHT VISION

Ophthalmosaurus's gigantic eyes suggest that it was able to see well in the dark. Like the eyes of modern-day giant squid (above), it is likely that they allowed it to travel hundreds of metres down to the dark zones of the ocean, looking for food.

One other ichthyosaur, Temnodontosaurus from England, had bigger eyes. However, it was a much bigger animal, so its eyes weren't as large compared to its body size.

Because eyes are filled with fluid, they don't change shape when an animal dives to great depth. The same is not true of the rest of the body. Organs become squashed and sometimes have to change position inside the body.

BIGGEST OCEAN EYES

Compare the size of Opthalmosaurus's eyes with two modern-day monsters of the deep.

1 ➡ **GIANT SQUID** ➡ 25cm WIDE
2 ➡ **OPHTHALMOSAURUS** ➡ 23cm WIDE
3 ➡ **BLUE WHALE** ➡ 15cm WIDE

Blue whale   Ophthalmosaurus   Giant squid

ALL IN THE EYES

We know Ophthalmosaurus had big eyes because the eye sockets in its skull (below) are huge – but we don't what shape its pupils were. Perhaps they were slit-shaped like some modern creatures with good night vision, such as cats. It's even possible they could have been square, like the pupils of some deep-diving penguins. Whatever shape they were, they would have got much bigger to let in light when Ophthalmosaurus was diving in deep, dark water.

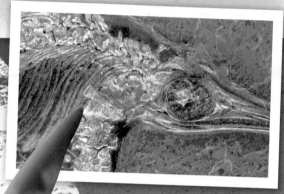

Ophthalmosaurus was a speedy, tuna-shaped predator. It had a powerful tail to propel it through the water.

 WORLDWIDE

Great eyesight helped to make Ophthalmosaurus a formidable hunter and to take advantage of the world's largest natural habitat – the ocean. That is why fossils of Ophthalmosaurus have been discovered worldwide, in areas that were covered by shallow seas during the Jurassic period.

OPHTHALMOSAURUS
(off-thal-moe-saw-rus)

WHEN	Jurassic 165-145 mya
WHERE	All around world
SIZE	4m long
WEIGHT	1 tonne
DIET	Fish, squid
SPEED	9km/h
DANGER	MEDIUM

OLDEST BIRD

ARCHAEOPTERYX

Fossils show us that birds evolved (developed) from small predatory dinosaurs – and since birds still exist today, we can say that dinosaurs are not extinct!

The oldest bird we know of is Archaeopteryx (ar-kee-op-ter-rix). Though it could probably fly and was covered in feathers, it was extremely similar to other small, feathered predatory dinosaurs and must have evolved from them.

EARLY BIRD

Archaeopteryx would have looked very different from modern birds. In fact, it probably looked more like a small version of feathery meat-eating dinosaurs such as Velociraptor. Its narrow jaws were lined with tiny teeth (left). It had long clawed fingers, a long feathered tail and a deep narrow body.

ARCHAEOPTERYX
(ar-kee-op-ter-rix)

WHEN	Jurassic 150-155 mya
WHERE	Germany
SIZE	50cm long
WEIGHT	500g
DIET	Carnivorous
SPEED	48km/h
DANGER	NONE

BORN TO RUN

Because Archaeopteryx has always been imagined as the 'first bird', it is often shown as a perching animal, similar in shape to a pigeon. In fact, its long hind legs and the shape of its toes and toe claws suggest that it ran quickly on the ground, with the second toes of its feet raised up off the ground. Perhaps it only flew when planning to cover large distances or when escaping from danger.

Fossils show that Archaeopteryx had big feathers on its arms and tail. Some experts think it also had long feathers on its hind legs, but this is harder to prove.

★ ★ ★ ★ KEY DIFFERENCES FROM MODERN BIRDS ★ ★ ★ ★

MODERN BIRD | ARCHAEOPTERYX

 VERSUS

MODERN BIRD	ARCHAEOPTERYX
★ TOOTHLESS BEAK	★ TOOTHED JAWS
★ FINGERS FUSED TOGETHER AND NO CLAWS OR SMALL CLAWS	★ LONG, SEPARATE FINGERS WITH BIG CLAWS
★ SHORT, STUBBY TAIL SKELETON	★ LONG, BONY TAIL SKELETON
★ SHALLOW, WIDE BODY SHAPE WITH VERY WIDE HIPS	★ DEEP, NARROW BODY SHAPE WITH NARROW HIPS
★ FIRST TOE ON FOOT OFTEN BIG AND POINTING BACKWARDS	★ FIRST TOE ON FOOT NOT FULLY TURNED BACKWARDS

Archaeopteryx probably had horny beak tissue around the edges of its jaws. But, unlike modern birds, it also had small teeth.

THE SURVIVORS

Archaeopteryx and other birds are dinosaurs. What makes birds different from other dinosaur groups is that they were the only group to survive the mass extinction that happened at the end of the Cretaceous, 65 million years ago. They probably survived because of their small size and ability to fly long distances.

Archaeopteryx lived on islands surrounded by a warm, shallow sea and might even have searched at the water's edge for dead fish and other prey.

LONGEST SPIKES

LORICATOSAURUS

Ferocious spikes more than a metre long sprouted from the tail of Loricatosaurus (lor-ee-cart-oh-saw-rus).

These are the longest spikes ever grown by any animal and were probably used to fight off enemies and impress mates.

SPIKY MYSTERY

When Loricatosaurus was alive, its spikes were even longer than the fossils that have been found - perhaps up to twice as long. This is because, like sheep's horns (below), the spikes weren't just made from bone, but were covered by a tough, horny sheath. This sheath was continually growing, but it does not survive in fossils, so we don't know how long it grew.

It's not clear exactly where all the spikes were on the body of Loricatosaurus. There may have been some on the shoulders or hips too.

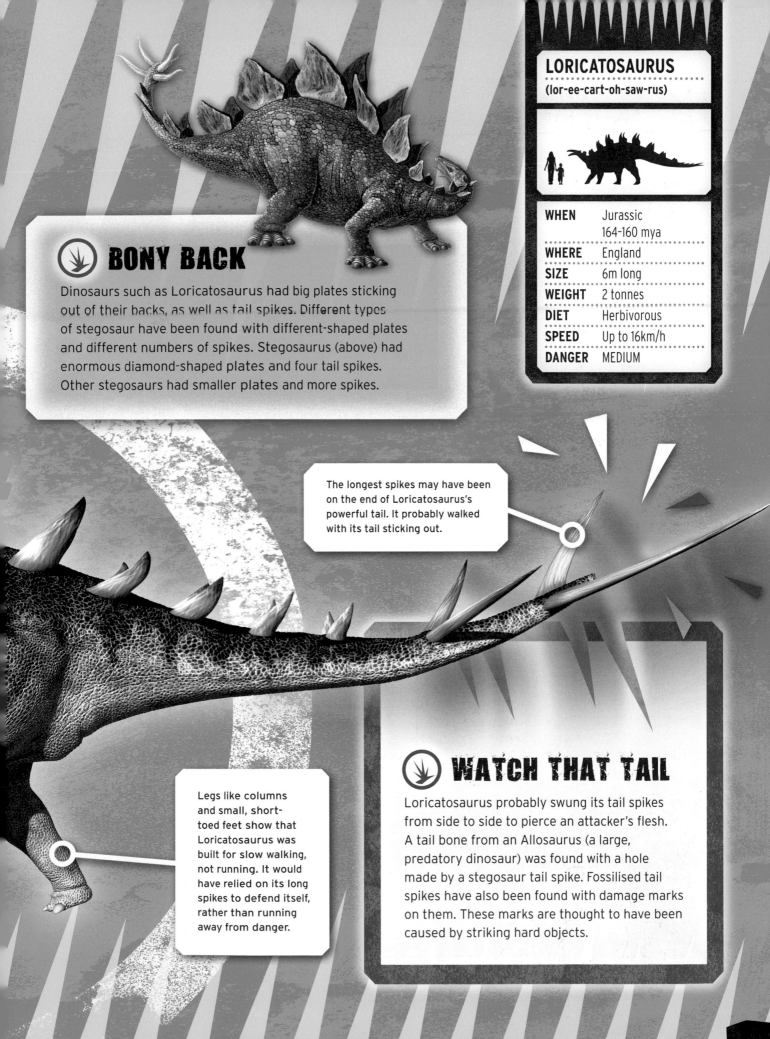

BONY BACK

Dinosaurs such as Loricatosaurus had big plates sticking out of their backs, as well as tail spikes. Different types of stegosaur have been found with different-shaped plates and different numbers of spikes. Stegosaurus (above) had enormous diamond-shaped plates and four tail spikes. Other stegosaurs had smaller plates and more spikes.

LORICATOSAURUS
(lor-ee-cart-oh-saw-rus)

WHEN	Jurassic 164-160 mya
WHERE	England
SIZE	6m long
WEIGHT	2 tonnes
DIET	Herbivorous
SPEED	Up to 16km/h
DANGER	MEDIUM

The longest spikes may have been on the end of Loricatosaurus's powerful tail. It probably walked with its tail sticking out.

Legs like columns and small, short-toed feet show that Loricatosaurus was built for slow walking, not running. It would have relied on its long spikes to defend itself, rather than running away from danger.

WATCH THAT TAIL

Loricatosaurus probably swung its tail spikes from side to side to pierce an attacker's flesh. A tail bone from an Allosaurus (a large, predatory dinosaur) was found with a hole made by a stegosaur tail spike. Fossilised tail spikes have also been found with damage marks on them. These marks are thought to have been caused by striking hard objects.

LONGEST NECK

OMEISAURUS

Omeisaurus (oh-may-saw-rus) holds the record for the longest neck of any dinosaur, compared to its body size.

A modern-day giraffe's neck is about twice as long as its body, but this dinosaur's neck was nearly 8.5 metres long. That's four times longer than its body.

The neck of Omeisaurus was so long compared to its body and tail that it seems surprising it didn't topple forwards.

LOADS OF BONES

Why did Omeisaurus have such a long neck? The answer lies in its skeleton. We have just seven bones, called vertebrae, in our necks. Most early dinosaurs had nine, but Omeisaurus had an impressive 17, which were also very long. Where other dinosaurs had back vertebrae, Omeisaurus had extra neck vertebrae, so its back was shorter and its neck was longer.

Omeisaurus had a big bony club at the tip of its tail. Perhaps it used this to whack approaching predators.

Its long, skinny neck must have lost a lot of heat. It would also have made Omeisaurus an easy target for big predators.

Long necks are great for reaching up high and looking around, but swallowing and pumping blood up to the head and brain are more of a problem. Omeisaurus must have adapted to cope with these problems, but we don't yet know how.

GIRAFFE-STYLE

Just like modern-day giraffes, Omeisaurus used its incredible bendy neck to reach up into tall trees for food. It could also move its neck a long way to either side and reach down to the ground, so it could pick and choose from lots of different plants.

LONG NECK LEAGUE TABLE

Omeisaurus takes the record for the longest neck compared to its body size, but other dinosaurs had longer necks.

1 → SUPERSAURUS → 16m LONG

2 → MAMENCHISAURUS → 12m LONG

3 → SAUROPOSEIDON → AT LEAST 11.5m LONG

4 → OMEISAURUS → 8.5m LONG

OMEISAURUS
(oh-may-saw-rus)

WHEN	Jurassic 164–160 mya
WHERE	China
SIZE	18m long
WEIGHT	8.5 tonnes
DIET	Herbivorous
SPEED	16km/h
DANGER	LOW

MOST SOUTHERLY DINOSAUR

CRYOLOPHOSAURUS

Cryolophosaurus (cry-oh-loaf-oh-saw-rus) was discovered in the frozen ground of Mount Kirkpatrick, Antarctica, just 650 kilometres away from the South Pole. This makes it the most southerly dinosaur ever found.

This new dinosaur was a mid-sized, two-legged predator with a strange crest on its head. Its name means 'frozen crested lizard'.

 ## JURASSIC ANTARCTICA

When Cryolophosaurus was alive, Antarctica was further north than it is today (above right). The world was warmer too, so there were no ice caps or freezing temperatures. Fossil trees show that Antarctica was forested then (above left) and must have been home to many different kinds of dinosaurs and other animals. The creatures that lived there would have had to cope with low (but not freezing) temperatures in winter.

CRYOLOPHOSAURUS
(cry-oh-loaf-oh-saw-rus)

WHEN	Jurassic 189-183 mya
WHERE	Antarctica
SIZE	6m long
WEIGHT	350kg
DIET	Carnivorous
SPEED	24km/h
DANGER	HIGH

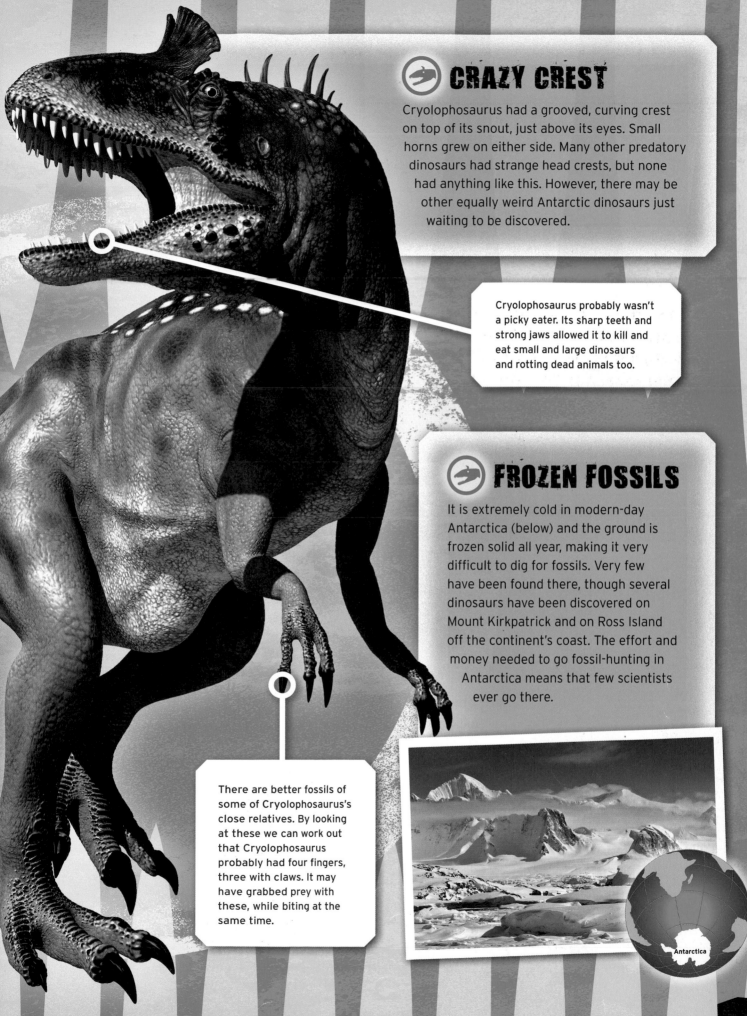

CRAZY CREST

Cryolophosaurus had a grooved, curving crest on top of its snout, just above its eyes. Small horns grew on either side. Many other predatory dinosaurs had strange head crests, but none had anything like this. However, there may be other equally weird Antarctic dinosaurs just waiting to be discovered.

Cryolophosaurus probably wasn't a picky eater. Its sharp teeth and strong jaws allowed it to kill and eat small and large dinosaurs and rotting dead animals too.

FROZEN FOSSILS

It is extremely cold in modern-day Antarctica (below) and the ground is frozen solid all year, making it very difficult to dig for fossils. Very few have been found there, though several dinosaurs have been discovered on Mount Kirkpatrick and on Ross Island off the continent's coast. The effort and money needed to go fossil-hunting in Antarctica means that few scientists ever go there.

There are better fossils of some of Cryolophosaurus's close relatives. By looking at these we can work out that Cryolophosaurus probably had four fingers, three with claws. It may have grabbed prey with these, while biting at the same time.

Antarctica

SMALLEST BRAIN

STEGOSAURUS

Most plant-eating dinosaurs had very small brains, but the brain of the giant-plated dinosaur Stegosaurus (steg-oh-saw-rus) was particularly tiny.

The brain of an adult human is about 25 times bigger! Very little of Stegosaurus's brain was actually used for thinking. Most of it was devoted to smell and other senses. In fact, the part used for thinking was about the size of a walnut.

⊙ SIMPLE STEGOSAURUS

The small brain suggests that Stegosaurus was mostly driven by instinct and that it didn't do much complicated thinking. But this is true of virtually all animals, so it's not as if Stegosaurus was at all unusual! Despite its tiny brain, Stegosaurus was not especially stupid. Most of the world's animals (like insects and fish) get by just fine with their small brains.

The part of the brain dealing with smell was quite large, so Stegosaurus must have been good at sniffing out tasty plants to eat.

TWO BRAINS?

An early idea about Stegosaurus was that a space in its spine housed a second brain, which was used to control the back half of its body. In fact, spaces like this are common in both large dinosaurs and modern birds and they don't house a brain. Instead, an organ called the glycogen body goes there.

WHEN	Jurassic 155-145 mya
WHERE	USA, Portugal
SIZE	7m long
WEIGHT	3.5 tonnes
DIET	Herbivorous
SPEED	16km/h
DANGER	MEDIUM

Stegosaurus would have relied on powerful sweeps of its huge tail to defend itself against predators, rather than brain power!

The glycogen body in the spine might have been an energy store, or it may have helped the animal control its balance.

SMALLEST BRAINS

Here are the top 5 dinosaurs with particularly small brains for their size.

1 → **STEGOSAURUS**
2 → **DIPLODOCUS**
3 → **KENTROSAURUS**
4 → **EUOPLOCEPHALUS**
5 → **TRICERATOPS**

BRAIN POWER

Predators tend to have bigger brains, as they need more brain power to hunt prey. Simple plant-eaters like Stegosaurus (right) didn't need as much brain power as cunning, fast-moving predators and so tended to have smaller brains for their body size.

MOST COLOURFUL

ANCHIORNIS

Anchiornis (an-kee-orr-nis), a small feathered dinosaur from China, is the most colourful dinosaur that we know of.

It had a reddish head crest, a mottled red and grey face, and striking patterns of black and white on its feathered wings and legs. Other non-feathered dinosaurs may have been more colourful, but we don't yet know for sure.

STRIKING CONTRAST

Anchiornis's body was mostly grey. The long feathers on its arms and hands were mostly white, but they had black tips and rows of black spots. Long leg feathers were also white and spotted with black. When Anchiornis spread its feathers and raised its crest, the result would have been striking, rather like a modern-day hoopoe.

COLOUR SECRETS

Experts can now work out the colours of feathered dinosaurs by studying the material in fossilised feathers that creates colour. Many feathered fossils have dark bands preserved across their surface, which represent the original pattern. Tiny cells called melanosomes, which help produce colours, are sometimes preserved too. It is not yet possible to find out this information for non-feathered dinosaurs.

⦿ NO BIRD

Anchiornis looked rather like a pigeon-sized bird. It had long arm, leg and tail feathers, a bushy crest and a covering of short body feathers. However, it also had features that birds don't have, such as a short blunt snout. In fact, it was actually a type of dinosaur called a troodontid and was related to the much larger Troodon (right).

The reddish crest – similar to that of many modern birds – may have been used in display, to impress mates.

The long arm and hand feathers would have mostly hidden the arm from view. Only the finger claws would have been visible.

ANCHIORNIS
(an-kee-orr-nis)

WHEN	Jurassic 165-155 mya
WHERE	China
SIZE	40cm long
WEIGHT	250g
DIET	Carnivorous
SPEED	Up to 40km/h
DANGER	NONE

Surprisingly, Anchiornis had feathers all the way down to the tips of its toes. Modern birds with feathery toes tend to live in cold places.

THE NEXT AGE OF DINOSAURS

After the Jurassic period ended, dinosaurs continued to rule the Earth for another 80 million years in the next phase of dinosaur evolution: the Cretaceous period.

New dinosaur species evolved while others died out, and by the part of the Cretaceous period known as the Campanian age (between 83 and 70 mya) there were as many as 100 different types. This is sometimes called the 'golden age of dinosaurs'.

Several giant meat-eating dinosaurs lived in Campanian North America, including Albertosaurus (left), Gorgosaurus and Daspletosaurus. Perhaps they avoided competing with one another by hunting different prey.

During the late Cretaceous age, high sea levels and flooding broke up the land into lots of smaller areas. The land animals split up across these different habitats and developed into new species.

Many Cretaceous dinosaurs lived on coastal plains, where there were clumps of trees and lots of low-growing shrubs and ferns. Others lived in densely wooded areas, marshes or lush forests.

Different species of duckbilled dinosaurs had different-shaped head crests. It would have been easy for each species to recognise its own kind by looking at these crests.

SHOW TIME

There were more dinosaurs with showy head-crests, incredible horns and fantastic frills in the Campanian age than at any other time in dinosaur history. Most of the crested duckbills, such as Parasaurolophus (above), and horned dinosaurs come from this time.

Horned dinosaurs from the Cretaceous age included short-frilled ones with long nose horns, like Styracosaurus, as well as long-frilled kinds with shorter nose horns, such as Pentaceratops.

BIGGEST MASS EXTINCTION

Sixty-five million years ago, at the end of the Cretaceous period, one of the most devastating mass extinctions of all time took place. It wiped out up to eighty per cent of all living things and ended the dinosaurs' reign on Earth.

One theory is that the extinction was caused by the effects of a massive asteroid (space rock) hitting Earth, but there is evidence that many groups of living things were not doing well, even before the asteroid hit.

During the Cretaceous period, shallow seas across the world dried up, destroying coastal areas and changing the climate and vegetation. These changes would have made life more difficult for the dinosaurs.

 ## MEGA EXPLOSION

A gigantic crater in Mexico, made about 65 million years ago, fits the asteroid theory. The Chicxulub crater is more than 180 kilometres wide and was created after a rock 10 kilometres wide slammed into Earth. It hit with a force 2 million times more powerful than the biggest explosion created by humans.

Towards the end of the Cretaceous period, up to two million cubic kilometres of lava poured out of volcanic cracks in India. This filled the atmosphere with toxic gases and perhaps changed the world's climate. This may also have contributed to the extinction event.

☄ ASTEROID IMPACT!

➡ ANIMALS AND PLANTS IN THE IMMEDIATE AREA OF THE BLAST ARE VAPORISED

➡ ANIMALS AND PLANTS WITHIN 1 KILOMETRE OF THE IMPACT ARE BURNED

➡ HEAT FROM THE BLAST CAUSES MASSIVE FIRES

➡ SHOCK WAVES CAUSE GIGANTIC TIDAL WAVES

➡ DUST THROWN INTO THE AIR BLOCKS OUT THE SUN FOR MONTHS, YEARS OR EVEN DECADES

➡ CHEMICALS BLASTED INTO THE ATMOSPHERE CAUSE ACID RAIN

The huge asteroid would have created a brightly glowing plume extending many kilometres up into the sky and would have vaporised on impact.

Sea creatures, marine and flying reptiles, and many groups of lizards and mammals were wiped out by the extinction event. The dinosaurs were badly affected too, but they did not all die off. One branch of the dinosaur family survived – the birds.

JURASSIC FACTS

Still want to know more about the Jurassic period? Here are more facts about the amazing creatures that lived in this time.

KNOW YOUR ERA

Although Tyrannosaurus rex features in movies such as *Jurassic Park*, it did not live in the Jurassic period. It evolved later, in the Cretaceous period.

BIGGER BONES

Some dinosaurs, especially meat-eaters, had internal air-filled sacs inside their bones, making them even bigger. It also makes their bones lighter than they look.

FOOT-SURE

Carnivores tended to have sharp claws on their feet, while herbivores had rounded toenails. Some even had feet like today's rhinos, elephants or pigs!

WHAT'S IN A NAME?

The word dinosaur means 'terrible lizard' in Ancient Greek. It was first used in 1842.

SMILE!

Dinosaur teeth grew continuously throughout their lives, like shark teeth today. If a dinosaur broke a tooth it could simply grow a new one. Some dinosaurs had over 1,000 teeth.

BIGGER, NOT BADDER

The biggest dinosaurs would never have preyed on smaller species, because they were herbivores. Only some of the smaller dinos were predators.

CHARGE!

Lots of the spikes and scales on dinosaurs, like those on Loricatosaurus, were for defence. Heavy herbivores couldn't run away if they were attacked, but they did need to protect themselves with their armour!

SNORKEL NOT NEEDED

The Apatosaurus (or Brontosaurus), a Jurassic sauropod, had nostrils on the top of its head. It could extend its incredibly long neck to breathe while standing deep in water.

OLD DINOS

It's thought that some dinosaurs may have lived for as long as 200 years.

ORIENTAL DRAGONS

Some of the most exciting dinosaur finds of recent years have been made in China. When Chinese people found a dinosaur tooth 3,500 years ago, before anyone knew anything about dinosaurs, they thought it belonged to a dragon.

LIFE CYCLES

Like birds and some reptiles today all dinosaurs laid eggs. They also created nests, and some dinosaurs are even thought to have taken care of their young once they hatched.

LONGEST REIGN

Dinosaurs ruled our planet for 165 million years. In comparison, humans have only lived for 2 million years.

CLEVER CREATURES

A newborn human baby has a bigger brain than most adult dinosaurs had. Whales and dolphins have the largest brains of all living animals today.

JURASSIC QUIZ

Test your knowledge with this fun quiz!
Find the answers at the bottom of the page.

1. What was the biggest land animal that ever lived?

a) Amphicoelias
b) Omeisaurus
c) Liopleurodon

2. How many vertebrae did Omeisaurus have in its neck?

a) 12
b) 7
c) 17

3. What colour was Anchiornis's feathery crest?

a) Red
b) Purple
c) Yellow and green stripes

4. How many brains did Stegosaurus have?

a) One
b) Two
c) Four

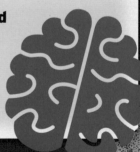

5. Did most dinosaur tails ...

a) ... drag along the ground like a lizard's?
b) ... stick out behind them in the air like a fox's?
c) ... wag floppily like a dog's?

6. Which dinosaur, unlike the others, used its tail as a whip?

a) Stegosaurus
b) Diplodocus
c) Fruitadens

44

7. Were Ophthalmosaurus's eyes the size of ...

a) ... a peach?
b) ... a grape?
c) ... a melon?

8. What sort of teeth did Liopleurodon have?

a) Slightly curved like bananas, with sharp points
b) Pencil-like
c) Leaf-shaped

9. How big was the smallest known predatory dinosaur?

a) About 10cm long
b) About 40cm long
c) About 100cm long

10. Why are Archaeopteryx fossils especially scientifically important?

a) Because they were well preserved
b) Because they are very rare
c) Because they show how birds evolved

11. Was Cryolophosaurus found ...

a) ... in Antarctica, near the South Pole?
b) ... in the Arctic, near the North Pole?
c) ... at the Equator?

12. When and where was Megalosaurus, the first dinosaur to be identified, discovered?

a) In Germany in 1845
b) In the USA in 1818
c) In England in 1824

ANSWERS

1=a, 2=c, 3=a, 4=a, 5=b, 6=b, 7=c, 8=a, 9=b, 10=c*, 11=a, 12=c   * All three answers are true, but (c) is the main reason.

45

GLOSSARY

Campanian
A section of the Cretaceous period, from 83 to 70 million years ago. This time period was the 'golden age of the dinosaurs'.

Carnivorous
The name given to creatures that kill and eat other animals in order to gain energy, and do not regularly eat plants. Sharks, tigers and Megalosaurus are examples of carnivorous animals.

Chicxulub crater
A giant crater in Mexico, 180km wide, created when a giant rock from space hit the Earth at the very end of the Cretaceous period. Despite its size it is not obvious, and it was only discovered during the 1970s.

Cold-blooded
The name given to animals that rely on heat sources like the sun to keep their bodies warm. The majority of living things are cold-blooded.

Crest
Any raised ridge of bone, feathers, fur or skin on an animal's head or body can be called a crest.

Cretaceous
The section of time (known as a period) between the Jurassic and Paleocene periods. It extended from 145 to 65 million years ago. Dinosaurs dominated life on land during the Cretaceous period.

Evolution
The tendency of all living things to change over time. Evolution usually happens over thousands of years, but we can also watch modern plants and animals evolve over short spans of time too.

Extinct
A living thing is extinct if it no longer exists. If an animal is described as extinct, it means that the last surviving one of the species has died.

Frill
The name given to the bony shelf that sticks out backwards and upwards from the skulls of horned dinosaurs like Triceratops. Frills were small in the earliest horned dinosaurs, but became enormous in later species.

Glycogen body
A rounded organ found between the two halves of the hips in many dinosaurs and modern birds. It may have acted as an energy store or even as an organ to help control balance.

Herbivorous
The name given to creatures that eat plants in order to gain energy and do not regularly eat animals. Herbivorous animals – called herbivores – tend to have large guts and a mouth suited to cropping plant material.

Ichthyosaurs
A group of swimming, marine reptiles from the Mesozoic period. Early kinds were shaped like lizards with flippers, but most of the best known ones were fish-shaped, with dorsal fins and shark-like tails.

Jurassic
The section of time (known as a period) between the Triassic and Cretaceous periods. It extended from 199 to 145 million years ago. Dinosaurs dominated life on land during the Jurassic.

Marine
A general term used for the area covered by seas and oceans, but also used to describe the plants and animals that inhabit this area. Sharks and whales are mostly marine creatures, and so were ichthyosaurs and plesiosaurs.

Mass extinction
An event in history when a large percentage of the animal and plant species alive at the time become extinct. Mass extinctions are caused by catastrophic events, such as a massive change in climate or the impact of a giant asteroid.

Mesozoic
The huge span of time (known as an era) that extended from 250 to 65 million years ago and included the Triassic, Jurassic and Cretaceous periods. The Mesozoic Era is often known as the 'age of reptiles': it is the time when dinosaurs ruled life on land.

Omnivorous
The name given to creatures that eat both animal and plant material in order to gain energy. Humans are omnivorous, and so are pigs and bears. The bodies of omnivorous animals combine plant-eating features and meat-eating features.

Ornithischians
The group of mostly herbivorous dinosaurs that possess a special bone in the lower jaw and back-turned hip bones. Stegosaurs, ankylosaurs and hadrosaurs are all ornithischians.

Palaeontologist
A scientist devoted to palaeontology – the study of ancient life. Palaeontologists tend to specialise in a particular part of palaeontology, such as fossil plants, dinosaurs or fossil marine reptiles.

Plesiosaurs
A group of swimming, aquatic reptiles from the Mesozoic era, all of which had two pairs of wing-like flippers. The group includes short-necked species with large heads as well as long-necked kinds with small heads.

Predator
A carnivorous (meat-eating) animal that survives by catching, killing and eating other animals. Wolves, tigers and sharks are all predators, but so are ladybirds and robins.

Pterosaurs
A group of winged reptiles, closely related to dinosaurs, that evolved in the Triassic period and died out at the end of the Cretaceous period. Pterosaurs had furry bodies and were probably warm-blooded.

Reptiles

The name usually given to the group of four-legged, scaly-skinned animals with a backbone that includes turtles, lizards, snakes and crocodilians. Most reptiles are cold-blooded, but some such as dinosaurs (including birds) and pterosaurs, were warm-blooded and furry or feathery.

Saurischians

The group of dinosaurs that possesses a particularly long, flexible neck, including both theropods (including birds) and sauropods and their relatives.

Sauropods

The group of long-necked, plant-eating dinosaurs that includes Diplodocus and Amphicoelias. Most sauropods were enormous and some kinds were the biggest land animals of all time.

Serrated

When the edge of an object possesses a set of tooth-like points like a saw, it is described as serrated. The edges of many leaves and the teeth of some carnivorous animals are serrated.

Triassic

The section of time (known as a period) between the Permian and Jurassic periods. It extended from 250 to 199 million years ago. Dinosaurs first appeared during the Triassic.

Vertebrae

The collective name for the bones that form the backbone – each of which is individually called a vertebra. Humans have 33 vertebrae, while long-bodied animals like snakes have more than 200.

Warm-blooded

The popular name given to animals that generate and keep heat inside their bodies. Mammals and birds are warm-blooded, but so are some insects and fish. There is evidence that at least some Mesozoic dinosaurs were warm-blooded.

INDEX

CREDITS

The publishers would like to thank the following sources for their kind permission to reproduce the pictures in this book. Every effort has been made to correctly acknowledge and contact the source and/or copyright holder of each picture, and Carlton Books Limited apologizes for any unintentional errors or omissions, which will be corrected in future editions of this book.

PICTURE CREDITS:

Dr Darren Naish, Corbis, Getty Images, istockphoto.com, Science Photo Library & Shutterstock.com